Babies' Names of Today

Babies' Names of Today

Kathy Randall O'Neal

To order additional copies of this book, contact:
Xlibris Corporation
1-888-795-4274
www.Xlibris.com
Orders@Xlibris.com
52941

Contents

Dedication

To my husband Robert O'Neal who supported this book and went the extra mile, you have been my supporter from the beginning. I will always cherish your support.

To my daughters Knartara Crittenden and Knarquelya O'Neal, you are my guiding lights that give me the inspiration to continue with my gift. Your patience made every moment worth the wait. More than that you taught me how to love and wait. To my granddaughters, Kanaja Sutton and Ta'lyn Crittenden, you are my future stars that live in my heart and to Erica Newton and Tunisia Newton, you are my future inspiration. I would like to give thanks to my special niece Cagina Randall-Spencer. Your leadership, drive and passion for your work have had an impact on my decision to pursue this book. Continue to strive for the best.

To my friend Polly Roberts, thank you for encouraging me to publish the names of all the babies I named. To Marlene Edwards my eight grade teacher, thank you for always telling me I had a gift. Most of all I would like to thank my late grandmother Mattie Randall, my mother Laura Mims and the late A.C Searles for always believing I can do all things through Christ who strengthens me.

To the best employer, Patricia Elder Thomas, thanks for believing I can be a great success.

Acknowledgement

I would like acknowledge my husband Robert, my family, my friends, God, and the mothers who named their children from my babies list. Thank you because you made me believe I had a special gift. The mothers are Margaret Ellis, Rowena Jackson (sister), Francine Randall (sister), Bernice Ellis-Bradford, Eva Ellis-Bell, Arthurene Spurlin-Crawford, Kathleen Toson, Oletha Coward (cousin) Gladys Stevens Hodge, Wanda Pooler (cousin), Vivian Pooler (cousin), Sheila James Wallace and Cagina Randall-Spencer (niece) and my teacher, the late Mr. Robert Cross. Thank you for wanting your children to have my special gift of names and making this creation possible.

About the Author

I was born in Albany, Georgia my family moved here before I was born. We lived in a neighborhood where everyone cared about each other. I was the third child born to my mother. As years passed my mother got married and moved. I was the only child that stayed with my grandmother Mattie Randall. My grandmother was a strict woman and had a lot of pride. I had to be in the yard before dark and had to go to school everyday. As a child I was fascinated with maps. I wanted to know how to spell every city, state and country on the map. I would sit daily and make-up baby names out of some of the cities and states. Daily as time went by I would play teacher with my sisters and friends. I would draw the map, study the map and make up names from the maps. I remember from the first grade to the ninth grade getting perfect attendance and staying on the honor roll. I knew then that studying played a great part in my life. After high school I attended college and later got married. Today, I have been married twenty-seven years with two daughters, Knartara and Knarquelya, one son-in-law, two granddaughters, two step children and three step grandchildren. Beside my grandmother, there were three very special teachers that inspired me, Mrs. Laura Blount, Mrs. Marlene Edwards, and Mr. A.C Searles. They would tell me use your gift and keep your head up because people will try to bring your head down. I was talking on the phone to a friend, Mrs. Polly Roberts about my daughter and she wanted to know where I got her name from (Knarquelya). I told her I made it up. I told her that I had named over 20 children. At that moment she asked me have you thought about publishing? For some reason as the year passed the thought came back to me about publishing and I said I always wanted to write a book. The conversation on the phone with my dear friend Polly sparked the book about baby names.

GIRL'S NAMES

1. Nae' Ja   (nay-ja)
2. Quanyee   (quan-ye)
3. Sardasha   (sar-dot-sha)
4. Shyasia   (shy-a-ya)
5. Shevokia   (she-vo-key-ar)

6.   Talaka   (tar-laka)
7.   Trastacia   (tra-stay-cia)
8.   Yasheka   (ya-she-ka)
9.   Knartara   (nar-tar-ra)
10. Knarquelya   (nar-kel-ya)

11. Ketronna   (key-tron-ar)
12. Karasha   (car-ra-sha)
13. Myquanna   (my-quan-na)
14. T'Myr   (t-mere)
15. Veshay   (v-shay)

16. Groshota   (gro-shot-ta)
17. Groshanta   (gro-shan-ta)
18. Laquanna   (la-quan-na)
19. A'Kiya   (ar-key-ya)
20. I "yette   (I'yette)

21. Shataya   (sha-tay-ya)
22. Markeltris   (mar-kel-tris)
23. Quanee   (quan-nee)
24. Niayarka   (nia-yar-ca)
25. Kretasia   (cre-tay-sia)

26. Rha'Shota   (ra-shot-ta)
27. I'Mese   (I-mese)
28. Sajada   (sa-jay-da)
29. Maryena   (mar-yen-na)
30. Jikenna   (ji-ken-na)

BOY'S NAMES

1. Sarterrance   (sir-tear-rance)
2. Laccardius   (la-car-de-us)
3. Shabertron   (shab-ber-tron)
4. Travinton   (tray-ven-ton)
5. Montralis   (mon-tral-lis)

6. Knatrallis   (na-tra-lis)
7. Yarkenzie   (yar-ken-zee)
8. Yarkenski   (yar-ken-ski)
9. Deyontis   (de-yon-tis)
10. Ventavious   (ven-tay-ve-ous)

11. Gromonde   (gro-mon-de)
12. Ventarious   (ven-tear-re-us)
13. Armonde   (ar-mon-de)
14. Kaquan   (ca-quan)
15. Armonte   (ar-mon-tae)

16. Traykee   (tray-key)
17. Laqualis   (la-qua-lis)
18. A'Jonte   (a-jon-tay)
19. Taymon   (tay-mon)
20. Arwante   (ar-wan-tae)

21. Donterrias   (don-tel-re-us)
22. Denetris   (de-ne-tris)
23. Fontaine   (fon-taine)
24. Dontaine   (don-taine)
25. Cajivis   (ca-ji-vis)

26. Zaykei   (zay-key)
27. Draynard   (dray-nard)
28. Tavee   (tay-vee)
29. Iyen   (I'yen)
30. Hikeyma   (hi-key-ma)

31. Nayarkis   (na-yar-kis)
32. Nakeem   (na-keem)
33. O 'Traya   (o-tray-ya)
34. Lavenja   (la-ven-ja)
35. Jalentae   (ja-len-tae)
36. Armarzo   (ar-mar-zo)
37. Rayvez   (ray-vez)

These babies names were picked from my list and the mothers and myself put the first and middle names together

Deyontis Traykee
Knartara Groshota
Knarquelya Groshanta
Karasha Arteka
Laccardius Gromonde
Montrallis A'Jonte
Makeltris Quanyae
Knartrallis Kaquan
Arshard Lonjuan
Sardasha Laquania
Sarterrance Laquallis
Tiacondra Sheiyarka
Shaterton Shanez
Talaka Lashay
Trastacias Quanee
Ventavious Taymon
Yarkenzie Arwante
Yarkenski Armonde
Yasheka Shakelle
Travintion Tradante'
Shevokia Iyette
Kanash Armeka
Denetris Fontaine
Donterrias Dontaine
Tayvee Jalente'
Starvincey Zayque

TWIN GIRL NAMES

1. Shy Asia Iyett   (shy-asia)-(I-yette)
2. T"Asia Aryette   (t-asia)-(ar-yette)

3. Talaka Lashay   (ta-lake-a)-(la-shay)
4. Delaka Lanay   (de-laka)-(la-nay)

5. MyQuanya Zanee   (my-quan-ya)-(za-nee)
6. JiQuanya Manee   (ji-quan-ya)-(ma-nay)

7.   Karasha Shalay   (car-ra-sha)-(sha-lay)
8.   Sardarsha Quanjay   (sar-dar-sha)-(quan-jay)

9.   Ketronna Maryae   (key-tron-na)-(mar-yae)
10.   Tetronna Ar'ye   (te-tron-na)-(ar-yae)

11. Delsha T'Myr   (del-sha)-(t-mere)
12. Kelsha V'Myr   (kel-sha)-(v-mere)

13. Hi'kema Yakeitris   (hi-key-ma)-(ya-key-tris)
14. Knarkema Taketris   (nar-key-ma)-(ta-key-tris)

15. De'Nata Monlette   (de-nata)-(mon-lett)
16. Zanata Yanlette   (za-na-ta)-(yan-let)

17. Lataelynn Jatese   (la-tay-len)-(ja-tese)
18. Shatelynn Jakese   (sha-tay-len)-(ja-kese)

BOY'S TWIN NAMES

1. Yakenski Rayvee   (ya-ken-ski)-(ray-vee)
2. Manenski Tayvee   (ma-nen-ski)-(tay-vee)

3. Donterrias Fontaine   (don-tear-re-us)-(fon-tane)
4. Lonterrias Dontaine   (lon-tear-re-us)-(don-tane)

5.   Tradante' Yarkese   (tra-dante)-(yar-keyse)
6.   Ardante' Zarkese   (ar-don-tae)-(zar-keyse)

7.   Denetris Zayketris   (de-ne-tris)-(zay-key-tris)
8.   DeKeytris Traykee   (de-key-tris)-(tray-key-tris)

9. Yarkenski Arvere   (yar-ken-ski)-(Ar-vere)
10. Yarkenzie Rayvere   (yar-ken-zie)-(ray-vere)

11. Deyontis Monquelle   (de-yon-tis)-(mon-quail)
12. Eyontis Donquelle   (e-yon-tis)-(don-kelle)

13.   Nayarkis Zymon   (nar-yar-kis)-(zy-mon)
14.   Keyvarikis Zytron   (key-var-kis)(zy-troon)

15.   Arcardius Quan-ye'   (ar-car-de-us)-(quan-yae)
16.   Decardius Juan-ye'   (de-car-de-us)-(juan-yae)

17. I'yen Arwante   (i-yen)-(ar-wan-te)
18. Kiyen Marwante   (ki-yen)-(mar-wan-tae)

19. Retroya Venkenski   (re-tro-ya)-(ven-ken-ski)
20. Detroya Zenkenski   (de-troy-ya)-(zen-ken-ski)

BOY AND GIRL
TWIN NAMES

1. Sardarsha Lawuanya Sarterrence Laquallis
2. Shyasia Tayeke Markasia Tyreke
3. Arkallis Quanee Knartrallis Monzae
4. Deyontis Taymon Y'Onis Shaayquan
5. Drekennon Tyrie Zarkenan Shyvica

www.ingramcontent.com/pod-product-compliance
Lightning Source LLC
Chambersburg PA
CBHW061223280526
45784CB00006B/2600